FUN WITH THE CLARINET

CONTENTS

Bb CLARINET FINGERING CHART

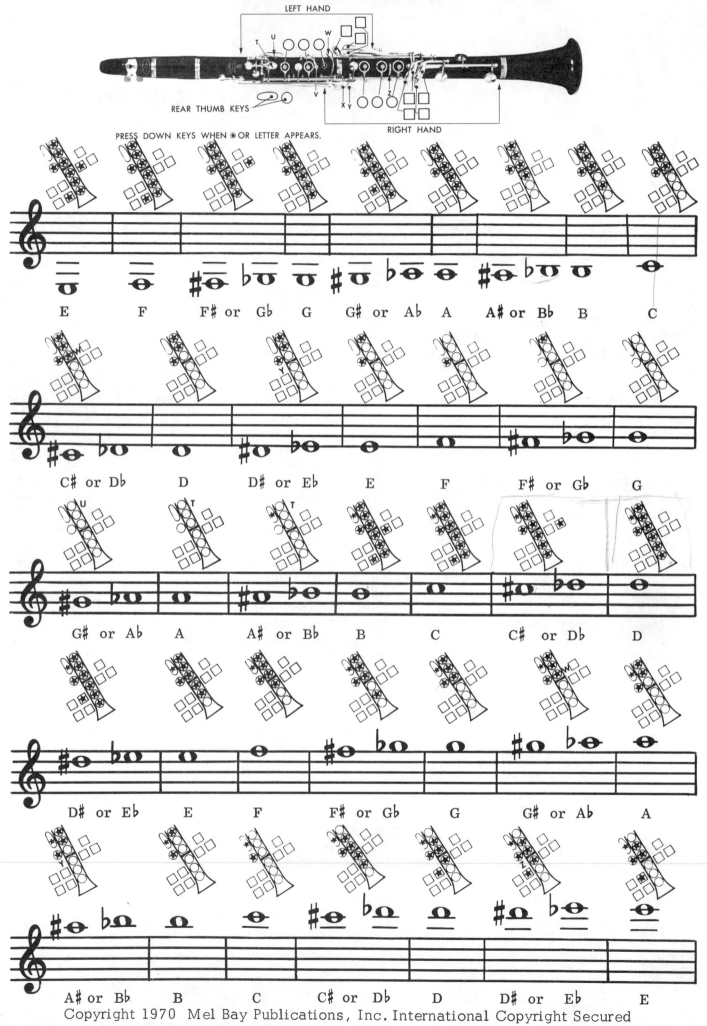

CAMPTOWN RACES

Moderately

Stephen Foster

When The Saints Go Marching In

Brightly

Traditional

FRANKIE AND JOHNNY

Moderately

Traditional

Black Is The Color Of My True Love's Hair

Slowly

Folk Song

BLOW THE MAN DOWN

Moderately

Sea Chanty

Michael Row The Boat Ashore

Spiritual

Moderately

RED RIVER VALLEY

Slowly

Cowboy Song

Drink To Me Only With Thine Eyes

Slowly   Traditional

TOM DOOLEY

Moderately

Folk Song

ALOUETTE

Brightly

French Song

AURA LEE

Slowly
Traditional

STREETS OF LAREDO

Moderately
Cowboy Song

OH! SUSANNA

Brightly

American Folk Song

Blue Bells Of Scotland

Scotch Folk Song

Look Down That Lonely Road

Spiritual

The Eyes Of Texas

Brightly

Traditional

THE ERIE CANAL

Brightly

Traditional

I've Been Working On The Railroad

Traditional

COCKLES AND MUSSELS

Folk Song

LOCH LOMOND

Moderately

Scotch Folk Song

HOME ON THE RANGE

Moderately

Cowboy Song

Chorus

WAYFARIN' STRANGER

Slowly

Folk Song

rit.

She'll Be Comin' 'Round The Mountain

Moderately

Traditional

mf

GREENSLEEVES

Old English Song

HATIKVOH

Moderately

Hebrew National Anthem

GYPSY LAMENT

Slowly

Gypsy Folk Song

Bill Bailey Won't You Please Come Home

Bright, With A Beat

Dixieland

Battle Hymn Of The Republic

Julia Ward Howe

Moderately

SHORTNIN' BREAD

Moderately

Traditional

COME BACK TO TORINO

Francesco Carlo Zucco

Bright Waltz

Swing Low, Sweet Chariot

SANTA LUCIA

Neapolitan Song

LONDONDERRY AIR

Slowly

Traditional

Down By The Riverside

With a strong beat

Traditional

Fine

Chorus

D.C. al Fine

Hail Hail The Gang's All Here

Moderately

Traditional

DIXIE

Brightly

Traditional

When Johnny Comes Marching Home

Moderately

Traditional

THIS TRAIN

Brightly

Spiritual

THE DRUNKEN SAILOR

Brightly

Sea Chanty

Chorus

I GAVE MY LOVE A CHERRY

Slowly

Folk Song

SHENANDOAH

Slowly

Folk Song

CAPE COD CHANTY

Brightly

Sea Chanty

Chorus

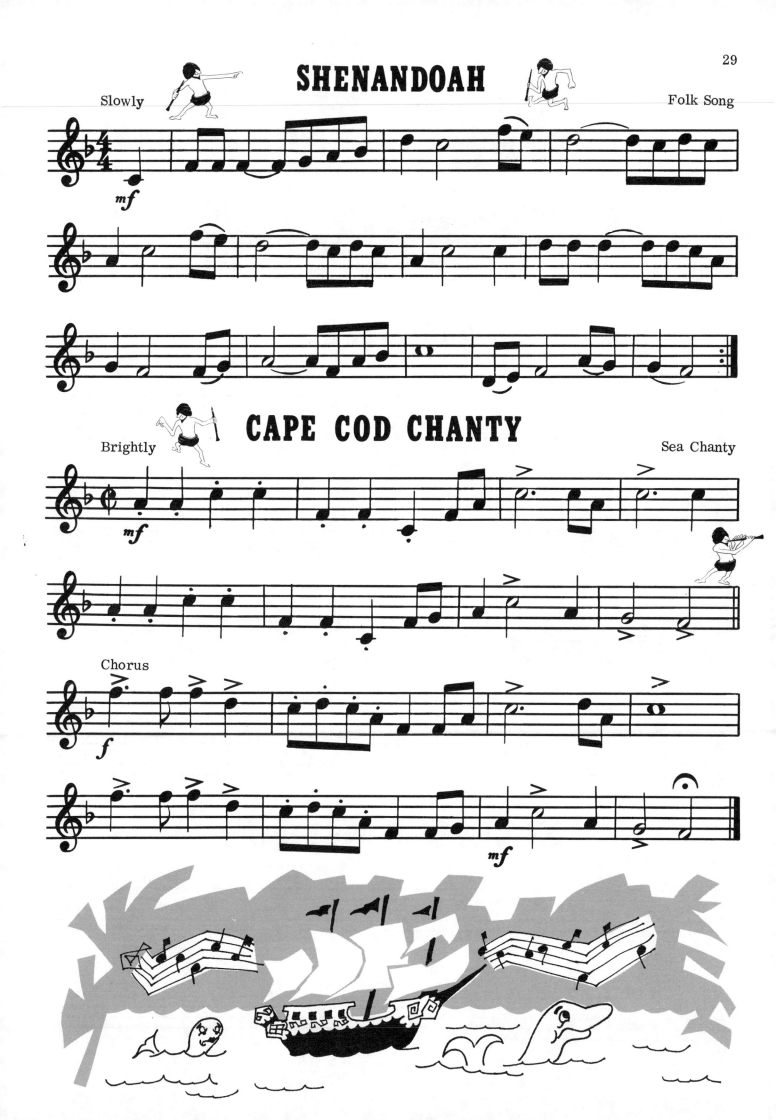

JOHN HENRY

Brightly

Folk Song

Old Shoe Boots And Leggins

Brightly

Traditional

It Takes A Worried Man

Brightly

Folk Song

THE ENTERTAINER THEME

Scott Joplin